# Material Detectives: Plastic

# Let's Look at the Frisbee®

## Angela Royston

**www.raintreepublishers.co.uk**
Visit our website to find out more information about **Raintree** books.

To order:
☎ Phone 44 (0) 1865 888112
🖹 Send a fax to 44 (0) 1865 314091
💻 Visit the Raintree Bookshop at **www.raintreepublishers.co.uk** to browse our catalogue and order online.

First published in Great Britain by Raintree, Halley Court, Jordan Hill, Oxford OX2 8EJ, part of Harcourt Education.
Raintree is a registered trademark of Harcourt Education Ltd.

Editorial: Andrew Farrow and Sarah Chappelow
Design: Jo Malivoire and AMR
Picture Research: Erica Newbery
Production: Duncan Gilbert

Originated by Modern Age
Printed and bound in China by South China Printing Company

ISBN 1 844 43430 3 (hardback)
10 09 08 07 06
10 9 8 7 6 5 4 3 2 1

**British Library Cataloguing in Publication Data**
Royston, Angela
Plastic: let's look at the frisbee – (Material Detectives)
620.1'923
A full catalogue record for this book is available from the British Library

**Acknowledgements**
The publishers would like to thank the following for permission to reproduce photographs: Michael Newman/Photo Edit p. **12**, **23** (girl); Punchstock p. **4**; The Image Works/TopFoto p. **19**; T Kaiser Henryk/Photolibrary p. **16**; Tony Freeman/Photo Edit p. **5**; Tudor Photography/Harcourt Education Ltd pp. backcover (melon and plate), **6**, **7**, **8**, **9**, **11**, **13**, **14**, **15**, **17**, **18**, **20**, **21**, **22**, **23** (all except girl), **24**; Wilmar Photography.com/Alamy p. **10**.

Cover photograph of the Frisbee® reproduced with permission of Tudor Photography/Harcourt Education Ltd.

Frisbee® is a registered trademark of ©2005 Wham-O Inc. CA, USA.

Every effort has been made to contact copyright holders of any material reproduced in this book. Any omissions will be rectified in subsequent printings if notice is given to the publishers.
The paper used to print this book comes from sustainable resources.

Some words are shown in bold, **like this**. They are explained in the glossary on page 23.

# Contents

# What is the Frisbee?

The Frisbee® is a toy.

You throw it through the air.

Another person can catch the Frisbee.

# What shape is a Frisbee?

A Frisbee is round and almost flat.

It is easy to hold.

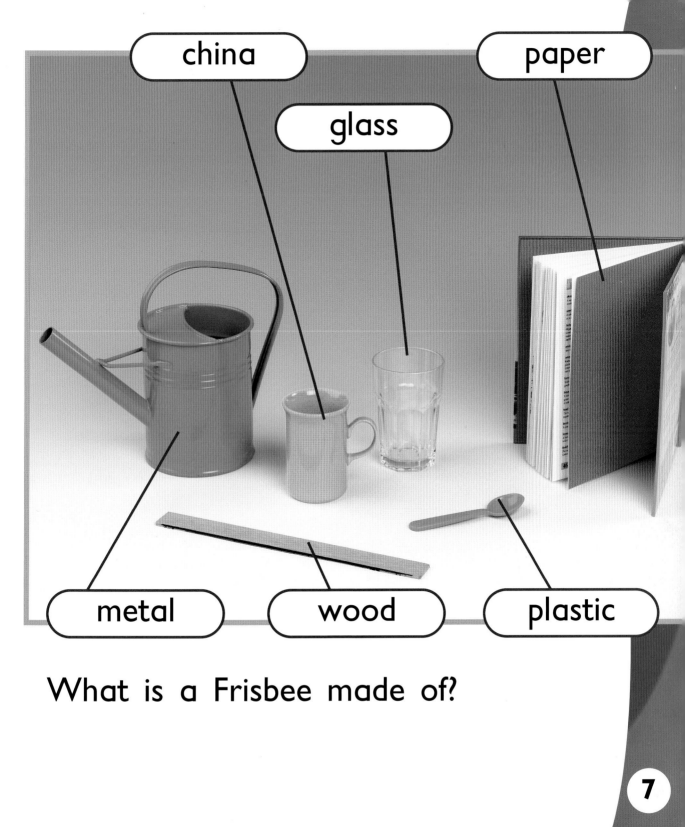

What is a Frisbee made of?

plate

ball

doll

kite

knife and fork

toy bulldozer

A Frisbee is made of plastic.

All of these things are made of plastic too.

Plastic can be made into any shape and colour.

Frisbees come in different colours.

# Is a Frisbee heavy or light?

Plastic is light.

This helps the Frisbee to fly.

Do you think a Frisbee is heavier or lighter than a **melon**?

A Frisbee is lighter than a **melon**.

It is easy to throw the Frisbee far.

It is not easy to throw a melon far.

It quickly drops to the ground!

# How strong is a Frisbee?

A Frisbee is **hard** and strong.

A Frisbee does not break if you drop it.

Which do you think is stronger –
a china plate or a Frisbee?

A Frisbee does not break easily.

You can throw it and drop it many times.

Don't drop a china plate.

It breaks very easily!

# Can you bend a Frisbee?

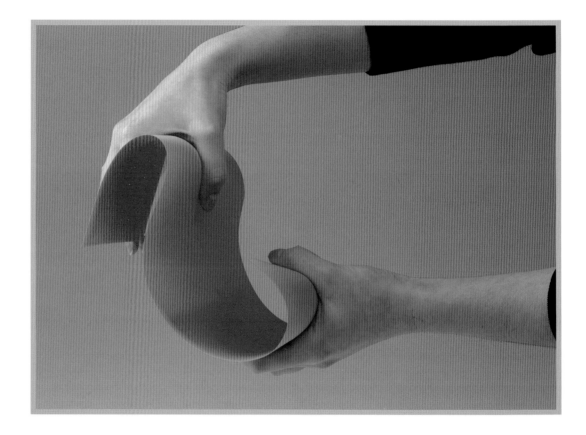

Is a Frisbee **bendy**?

Can you fold it like a sheet of paper?

A Frisbee is **rigid**, like a piece of wood.

This makes it fly better.

# How long will a Frisbee last?

Water will not harm a Frisbee.

Plastic does not **rust**.

Plastic does not **rot** like wood.

Things made of plastic last a very long time.

# Quiz

Which of these things are made of plastic?

Look for the answer on page 24.

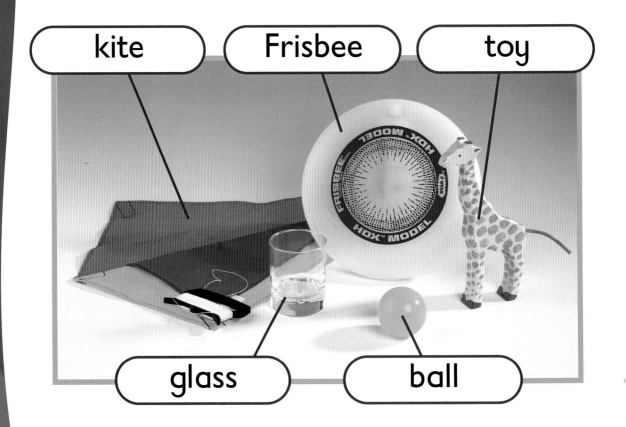

kite

Frisbee

toy

glass

ball

# Glossary

**bendy**
easy to bend or fold

**hard**
not soft, so you cannot squash it

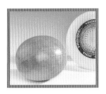

**melon**
a kind of fruit

**rigid**
stiff and hard to bend

**rot**
go bad and break down into little pieces

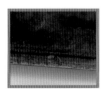

**rust**
when metal slowly turns orange and crumbles

# Index

Answers to the quiz on page 22

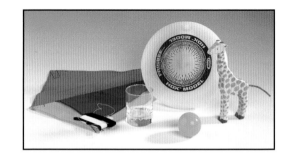

The Frisbee, kite, and ball are all made of plastic. The toy is made of wood and the glass is made of glass.

## Note to parents and teachers

Reading for information is an important part of a child's literacy development. Learning begins with a question about something. Help children think of themselves as investigators and researchers by encouraging their questions about the world around them. Each chapter in this book begins with a question. Read the question together. Look at the pictures. Talk about what you think the answer might be. Then read the text to find out if your predictions were correct. Think of other questions you could ask about the topic, and discuss where you might find the answers. Assist children in using the picture glossary and the index to practice new vocabulary and research skills.

# Titles in the *Material Detectives* series include:

Hardback          1 844 43429 X

Hardback          1 844 43430 3

Hardback          1 844 43636 5

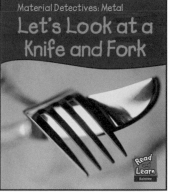

Hardback          1 844 43428 1

Hardback          1 844 43427 3

Hardback          1 844 43634 9

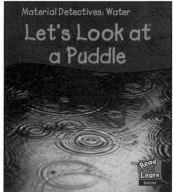

Hardback          1 844 43635 7

Hardback          1 844 43637 3

Find out about other titles from Raintree on our website www.raintreepublishers.co.uk